First published 1985

ISBN 0 906520 22 3

© Middleton Press, 1985

Phototypeset by   CitySet Ltd, Chichester.

Published by   Middleton Press
                Easebourne Lane
                Midhurst, West Sussex.
                GU29 9AZ

Printed & bound by   Biddles Ltd.,
                      Guildford and Kings Lynn.

COVER PICTURE: Out into the sunshine from Brighton station's great roof, the Birkenhead – Hastings train sets off for Eastbourne in the spring of 1953, when SR carriages still carried full roofboards. K class no.32352 is in charge.

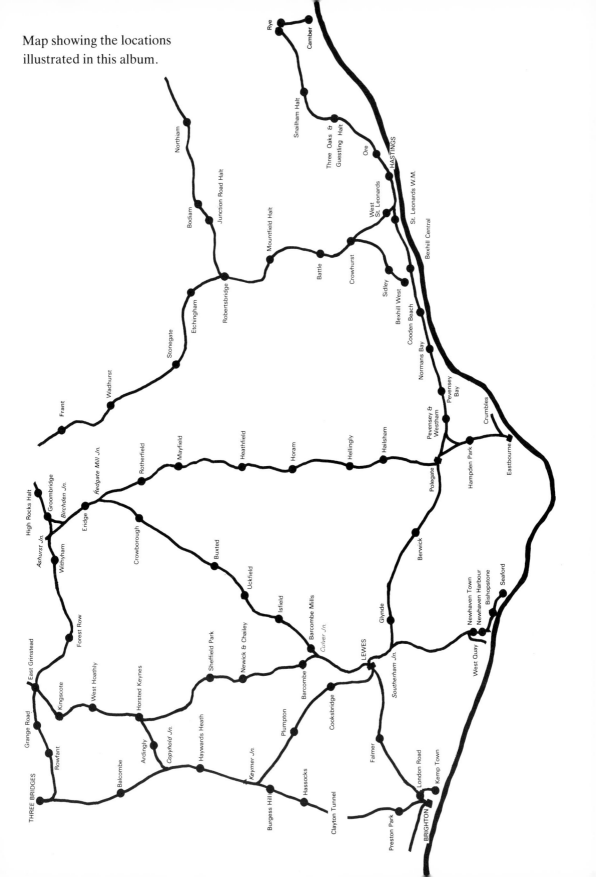

Map showing the locations illustrated in this album.

CONTENTS

INDEX

INTRODUCTION

This book began as a companion to my book *Steaming Through Kent* (Middleton Press), as a celebration of the age of steam in Sussex. As with Hampshire, there turned out to be such a wealth of material that two books are needed to do it justice. This first volume covers the eastern part of the county with the main line to Brighton as its western boundary but includes pictures of trains on that main line.

The pictures are arranged in six sections which are listed in the Contents and within each section we move along the lines involved, in station order. I have not provided a detailed history of the routes covered because the information is readily available elsewhere, but the outline is this. Brighton was an obvious goal for railway promoters and the London & Brighton Railway line from London was the earliest main line in the county. Another obvious move was to build westwards towards Kent tapping the potential of Hastings on the way. Kent however was the territory of the South Eastern Railway, and after some argument St. Leonards became the boundary between the two companies. In 1851 the SER invaded Sussex with a direct line to Hastings, from its main line at Tonbridge south through Tunbridge Wells. The LBSCR which had been formed in 1846 by amalgamation of, among others, the London & Brighton and the Brighton, Lewes & Hastings Railways, spent the rest of the century keeping the SER from further incursions into Sussex. This was achieved by building lines to occupy the area within the triangle Three Bridges – Brighton – St. Leonards. Some of these lines were promoted locally; all fell into the 'Brighton' net sooner or later.

There were two new developments around the turn of the century. One was the building of the SECR line from Crowhurst to Bexhill where it came up against the LBSCR, well established in the town. The other was the building of the Rother Valley Railway from the Hastings line towards Tenterden in Kent. It was a typical Col. Stephens affair. Railway lovers will know what that means, and readers who don't can easily find out by looking at the pictures of it in section six.

In 1923, the LBSCR and the South Eastern & Chatham Railway – as the SER after its shotgun marriage with the London, Chatham & Dover Railway was called – were amalgamated into the Southern Railway, and then nationalised in 1948. Thereafter, though not as a result, the rot set in. Cars, lorries, and buses took much of the railways' business away and by the 1950s many of the quieter lines were doomed. These pictures were often taken in an attempt to record the branches coming under the axe before it fell, though there have been some surprising reprieves and resurrections. The tragi-comedy of the Sheffield Park line in the late 1950s is recounted in *Branch Lines to East Grinstead* (Middleton Press), but the record of railway preservation in East Sussex is happier, with the Bluebell and the Kent & East Sussex Railways flourishing, and the Lavender Line starting at Isfield in 1984. All these are faithful to steam.

I have tried to make the captions informative and accurate though I dare not claim to be an authority. That role belongs to the sages of The Brighton Circle, to whom I am much indebted for a lot of the detailed information which I have included. Their *Circular* is a mine of information, arcane and hilarious. I'm also sure that your careful scrutiny of these pictures will reveal details I don't mention. The views are mainly at stations, which I know is welcome to the modellers, and probably more interesting to my fellow residents in East Sussex as showing familiar scenes as they used to be. If you want to get more information, there is no shortage of published material. Following on from the reprinted *History of the Southern Railway* by C.F. Dendy Marshall, there is also a three volume history of the LBSCR by J.T. Howard Turner. The SER still awaits similar detailed treatment, but more general accounts are to be found in the books by H.P. White and Dr. E. Course, both of which cover East Sussex. On signalling, locomotives, and rolling stock we have been well served by George Pryer, D.L. Bradley and P.J. Newbury. Lastly there are the Middleton Press companions to this book: *Branch Lines to East Grinstead, Branch Line to Tenterden* and *South Coast Railways – Brighton to Eastbourne*.

I have tried the patience of quite a few people in Sussex libraries and museums in gathering these pictures together. I hope you like also the odd non-railway and non-picture items. Of the photographs, the more recent work is either my own or of others whose names are given in the captions, and I offer them all my thanks for their co-operation in allowing their work to be used. Older pictures which are not credited are from my own collection. Lastly, Neil Stanyon read the proofs as usual, earning my thanks and yours for his efforts.

Peter Hay
Hove 1985

1 THE MAIN LINE: THREE BRIDGES TO BRIGHTON

Although the total distance from London to Brighton is only 50 miles, less than half of which is in Sussex, the route has never been anything but a main line, and to 'Brighton' men, *the* Main Line. Photographers have covered it assiduously and electrification in 1932 didn't banish steam by any means, as these pictures show. Only recently has steam's speed record for the journey been beaten, though the trains you will see here were not doing any racing. The two well known civil engineering works, over the Ouse valley and under the South Downs, are both pictured but mostly I have tried to choose views of stations. These have altered a lot in recent years so perhaps some memories of things as they used to be will be awakened.

Unlike the trains photographed on the other lines in this book the modern pictures in this section are all of extra or 'dated' trains, because in the 1950s there were only two timetabled steam passenger workings by day, the Birkenhead - Hastings service in each direction between Redhill and Brighton. I make no apology for the fact that only passenger trains are shown, for this always was and remains primarily a passenger line. When it was built in 1840 it was as the direct route to Brighton. There were no places of any size on the way and centres like Haywards Heath and Burgess Hill have grown up because of being on the railway. Indeed the latter isn't even mentioned on an 1813 map, whereas Horsted Keynes for example is shown as an established settlement. Railways have influenced East Sussex a lot, the main line more than any other.

1. The busier northern half of the main line from London to Brighton was widened to four tracks before World War I. Through Three Bridges the fast lines were slewed to the east, acquiring the slight kink seen on the left of this picture in order to continue using the existing bridge over the Crawley - East Grinstead road and the existing down platform. Even at today's speeds passengers hardly notice the kink. This train was going slowly as it moved into the station to work a tour round some Sussex branches in 1953. The engine with the LBSCR 'motor' set is the last D3 class 0–4–4 tank, no.32390.

2.   Balcombe station has not changed much from this late Victorian view though the platforms are longer now and the footbridge is concrete, but there is still the feeling of being deep in the country. The train which everyone in sight is ignoring looks like an excursion returning from London behind a 'Grasshopper': one of Billinton's B2 class 4–4–0s.

3. Under threatening skies on a showery 1962 day a railtour from London to the Bluebell Railway crosses the great viaduct over the Ouse valley. This picture was taken from one of the stone pavilions which adorn the ends of the structure, and the engine with steam to spare as it coasts down from Balcombe tunnel is a former Great Northern Railway saddletank, which is at present on loan to the National Railway Museum.

4. Haywards Heath station was completely rebuilt for the electric services which began in 1932, and was equipped with colour light signals and one signal box in place of two. The former north box and its signals can just be seen above the leading carriage of this 1930 vintage Eastbourne express, headed by an H2 class Atlantic no.B421 *South Foreland*. The number 114 on the engine is to help signalmen to identify individual trains during heavy holiday traffic. (H.C. Casserley)

6. The station with a train passing through was a standard scene for producers of local postcard views in the 1890s. Taking the picture was such a novelty that everybody in it was usually watching the photographer. This is Burgess Hill, in the last Victorian years by the look of the ballast covering the sleepers. The ragged white line half way up the face of the opposite platform is the top edges of the stone blocks used to make it. They were the stone sleepers from the original main line of 1841, and they later had brickwork placed on top to bring the platform height up to standard.

←

5. South of Haywards Heath between Wivelsfield and Burgess Hill is Keymer Junction where the line to Lewes goes off eastwards. It is the route of the Newhaven boat trains. This one, bound for Victoria, has been stopped to allow a down electric train to clear the junction. No.32426 *St. Albans Head* is another of the Brighton Atlantics, a class that was associated with Newhaven shed and the boat train workings for many years. (A.J.K. Wadmore)

7. This picture of Hassocks Gate station in the 1870s shows the original height of the gravelled platforms when built of old stone sleepers. We are looking south, with the goods yard at the far end of the station and the Clayton 'notch' on the skyline above the tunnel. The modest building was retained in the major reconstruction of 1880 which also saw 'Gate' dropped from the name, but it was all swept away in 1972 for the dreary bus shelter style.

←

8. Fifty years later the platforms have been built up to modern height and asphalted. The train is the all-Pullman 'Southern Belle' to Brighton, hauled by B4 class 4–4–0 no.48. There is a Billinton bogie van for the luggage followed by six Pullmans, mainly 12-wheelers. Informative station nameboards were necessary in the days when everyone travelled by train. (Brighton Library)

9. The famous turreted north portal of Clayton tunnel did not originally have a cottage between the towers: that was added in 1849 for a lavish outlay of £65. It was still inhabited in 1953 when no.34047 *Callington* was caught heading north with one of the Saturday through trains to the Midlands.

10. Like Hassocks, Preston Park has suffered the bus shelter treatment, though once it even had a separate booking office at street level. As a result of further changes in 1985 the down loop line on the left has been taken out of use but the lead to the sidings on the right is still there. U1 class 2–6–0 no.31893 is just passing the site of the north signal box abolished in 1932, as it tackles the climb to Clayton tunnel with a heavy train to Wolverhampton.

11. The 1950s was the 'Indian summer' of the Brighton Atlantics and here we see no.32425 *Trevose Head* running fast on the final approach to Brighton with one of the summer Saturday through trains from the Midlands. The scene is on the short five-track section south of Preston Park. This train is on the down main while the tracks on the left lead to Hove and the West Coast line.

BRIGHTON AND NORTH WESTERN RAILWAYS.

(166 - 31 N.W.)

SUNNY SOUTH EXPRESS.

BRIGHTON
TO
BIRMINGHAM

W. & S. Ltd.

12. The pioneer 'Schools' class no.30900 *Eton* setting out from Brighton for Eastbourne with the 10.40am from Birmingham Snow Hill via the Western Region route through Reading. The carriages are GWR, now doubtless gone, like the locomotive works on the left, but Brighton station's great roof survives.

Work started on a line east from Brighton soon after the trains started running from London, though the South Downs drove the route inland until it reached Pevensey. How would Lewes have fared if there had been no cliffs to bar the way of a coastal route? As it turned out the hills forced the railway through Lewes, though not without difficulty, and its position became as strategic to the LBSCR defence of Brighton as it had been to the Normans in their control of East Sussex. East of Lewes the line threw off a branch to the major Sussex port of Newhaven, which was developed by the Newhaven Harbour Company (Offices: London Bridge Station, London). It was later brought into full railway ownership. Further east, both nascent Eastbourne and established Hailsham got single line branches, but the goal was Hastings, where a snappish confrontation with the SER in the 1850s settled down to peaceful competition until the amalgamation in 1923. In time the built-up area along the coast around Hastings acquired nine stations and halts, with the balance of power shifting from the LBSCR to the SECR as one went eastwards. There was some sort of parallel with the situation at Portsmouth, between the LBSCR and the LSWR.

In 1935 the electrics came, the wooden motor halts were rebuilt in concrete, especially Cooden for which great things were hoped, and for the East Coast line, The Southern Electric had arrived. Looking at these pictures of steam days east of Lewes I am tempted to add 'and nothing was ever the same again'. Then I remember that brief hot summer when I was Stationmaster at Pevensey, and how that was still a country station. How the sheep were sheared beside the platform at Pevensey Bay. How the two brothers who together ran Normans Bay, one early turn and one late, lived with their parents in the railway house beside the line by the crossing. I was anxious about the security of the rather modest station cash after the last train but I need not have worried. When I asked them what they did with it at night they said 'We take it home to Mum'. It was the same railway, electrics or not.

Beyond Hastings was the deep country of the county march and the approach to the great wide marshes. There were more halts and the charming Rye & Camber Tramway, but little traffic compared with further west, and still less after buses and cars appeared on the roads in quantity. Had it not been a through route of some operating importance the line from Hastings to Ashford would have become a 'thin end' or a 'withered arm' and must have perished in the recent slaughter of such loss-makers. But it is still delightfully with us, defended repeatedly and successfully by people who want their railway.

13. Steam trains from Brighton through Lewes mostly used the eastern platforms at Brighton, like No. 9 from which this train is leaving. No. 10 beyond it, the sidings with the 'Birdcage' brake, and the locomotive works buildings in the background, are now all part of the station car park. Underneath the wooden platform 8 on the right is a roadway built for horse cabs, too sharply curved at its north end for any taxi ever to negotiate.

14. From a vantage point above the main line to London we see the great sweep of the viaduct bringing the railway from Lewes into Brighton. The arches just visible at the tangent of the curve were destroyed by a German bomb in 1943 but faithfully rebuilt, balustraded parapet and all. The wagons in the foreground stand on a level with the main line, and behind them at a lower level and out of sight, runs the incline down to Brighton Lower Goods Yard passing beneath the viaduct. In April 1959 the evening Tonbridge to Brighton train was headed by 31470, an SE&CR class D1 rebuild, with Maunsell coaches. London Road station is in the distance to the right of the exhaust.

15. Most of the Brighton - Tonbridge trains in the 1950s were worked by former SECR 4–4–0s, but sometimes there was a shortage and a C class goods was turned out for duty, as on this day in September 1953. No. 31716 was an unusual member of the class because it had a Westinghouse brake pump (next to the cab) as well as the usual steam reverser between the splashers. London Road station looks a lot barer now, without its awnings and gaslights.

16. Kemp Town Junction is amply illustrated in the *Brighton to Eastbourne* volume of the South Coast Railways Series, so this picture of a 'Coppertop' (SECR class D) shows the now lifted siding into the Brighton Municipal Abattoir.

→

18. Kemp Town yard was usually deserted with just the daily goods to disturb the quiet. The tunnel is still there, blocked at the far end, and now used as a rubbish dump. Engine no.31727 from Tonbridge is filling in time between passenger workings.

London Brighton & South Coast Railway.

Hailsham to

Kemp Town

17. From time to time, a railtour thronged the single platform at Kemp Town with passengers, as in 1956 when there was still a useful daily freight business in coal and biscuits. Beyond the open doors of the containers on the left, the maltings of Willett's (later the Kemp Town) Brewery were still in existence. The engine is the Stroudley liveried Brighton Works shunter.

19. Not all old engines were dirty in the 1950s. Tonbridge generally managed to keep theirs fairly clean, as we can see from D1 class 31487 which is seen passing Falmer with an evening train, in May 1957. This small station has since had glory thrust upon it with the opening of Sussex University, nearby on this side of the line, and of part of Brighton Polytechnic opposite.

20. Looking towards Brighton from under the footbridge at Lewes, in October 1956. Beyond the overbridge the start of the climb to Falmer can just be seen and D1 class 31487 is blowing off after coasting down the bank. Immediately above the tender is the iron tank supplying the many water cranes. It was in fact outside the railway boundary, on the far side of the station approach road. Lewes also had, in the 1950s, no less than four Refreshment Rooms, so every need was catered for. The platform seat is ex-LBSCR.

21. This picture of a Tonbridge to Brighton train leaving Lewes in the winter of 1956 was taken from the steps of Lewes South signal box, and shows the up home signals which were in fact platform starters. By this date they were SR upper quadrant pattern, but still on a genuine LBSCR gantry, now preserved. In the distance is the main junction, between the lines to Culver and Southerham Junctions, while on the left we get a glimpse of the 1889 station building with its variegated brickwork. The loop line immediately in front of the buildings was closed in 1971 and the track space partially filled in. Eastbound trains originating from Lewes often started from there, and its curvature was such that the 1922 Appendix to the Working Timetable ordered: 'The L&NW Through Train must on no account be run into the Down Brighton Loop Line'.

22. If the signalman at Lewes Main Junction had time to step outside for a breath of air in October 1956, this is what he would have seen: an LBSCR 'Vulcan' no.32521 blowing off impatiently as it pulled out of platforms 4/5 with the 9.30am to East Grinstead, the first of the four daily trains of the 'sulky service'. There were so few passengers that the motor set was soon reduced to a single coach.

23. N class 2–6–0 crossing Southerham bridge with Eastwood's cement works behind. The engine's tender is on the lifting span, with Southerham Junction to the right and Lewes East Yard to the left.

24. Standing on the siding between Southerham Junction and Eastwood's cement works is the engine that assisted the one seen in picture 72 of *Brighton to Eastbourne*. It is *Atlas No.17*, surprisingly almost the same age as the little Andrew Barclay but looking much more powerful, which is understandable as it came from a steelworks. It was Hawthorn Leslie no.2532.

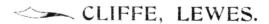

25. After the East Coast line east of Lewes crossed the Ouse (picture 23) it split into two parallel pairs of lines, one for Polegate and the other for Newhaven and Seaford. The short goods train behind the K mogul has come from Newhaven, having called at Asheham cement works on the way: hence the two brake vans. Today the junction is at the far end of the cutting and these Newhaven lines are just sidings. Note the signal wires routed along the top of the bank on the right, rather than at track level.

26. This double headed boat train was a result of the Coronation: the electric engine which normally covered the scheduled services was working special trains to the Fleet Review at Spithead on 14th June 1953. Unwilling or unable to provide a Pacific, the Loco Department turned out nos.31892 and 31504, a U1 2–6–0 and a D1 4–4–0, for this heavy train. The picture was taken from the steps of Newhaven Town North signal box, provided, like the sidings, to cope with extra traffic to the Western Front in World War I.

27. This curious scene at Newhaven Town station requires some explanation. The train is a rail tour from Victoria headed by the last surviving Brighton Atlantic no.32424 *Beachy Head*. After working to the Newhaven marine platforms it was pulled back to the Town station with, properly, a tail lamp on the engine now in the rear. Then we all got out to have a walk round the engine shed before returning to London via Brighton. Today this view would include the coast road flyover which replaced Newhaven's notorious level crossing.

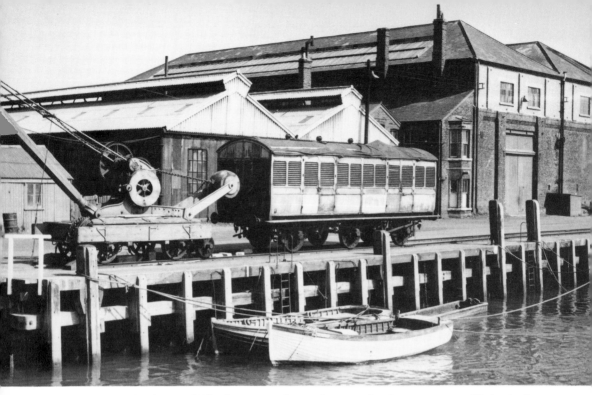

28. Standing in front of Newhaven engine shed (corrugated iron) and the Marine Workshops (brick) are two relics of the LBSCR. On the left is an ancient hand crane, all chains and baulks of timber. Notice the brackets folded against the underframe to support the hinged longitudinal platform. Was it for the crane gang to stand on as they wound the beast? The LBSCR, hampered in its pursuit of passenger traffic by its long sea crossing to France, competed very hard for continental freight business. Next to the crane is a Grande Vitesse van of 1906-08, The GV Service, as it was called, promised a guaranteed onward transit each day. There was also a Petite Vitesse service, naturally slower.

29. One of Newhaven's railway delights was the West Quay tramway which crossed the river by a swingbridge dating from 1866. Its wooden deck also carried the coast road. Only 'Terrier' class engines were allowed across and here no.32662 is coming back from a trip on the tramway, while road traffic quite properly is being held back to allow its cautious progress. The date is February 1960, three years before the tramway closed. The cranes are on the North Quay beyond the bridge.

30. Looking across Newhaven harbour we see a 'Terrier' pushing two trucks towards the West Breakwater area of the tramway. Prominent behind the train is the Victorian fort which never had to withstand a siege. Did the Newhaven Harbour Co. (who once worked the trains) run a special over the tramway to bring ammunition for its guns, or did their original stock last out until they were withdrawn?

31. The Wallis Patent Expansion engine was the property of A.F. Skinner, haulage contractor of Newhaven, according to the caption on this Edwardian postcard. It is seen approaching the swingbridge from the Town station, the West Quay tramway rails between its wheels, while pulling a new boiler for a local silica crusher, the movement needing a large number of flat caps for success. The engine was built by Wallis & Steevens of Basingstoke about 1900. (Newhaven Local & Maritime Museum)

33. A Victorian boat train in the excellent shelter of the marine platforms at Newhaven, no doubt a welcome sight after a rough crossing. The oil-lit carriages and the signals slotted through the post (with the lamps separate from the arms) suggest a date about 1890. Down the train, a Pullman car lords it over humbler vehicles but even it cannot outshine no.192 *Jacomb Hood*, one of Stroudley's famous 'Gladstone' class.
(G.F. Burtt)

32. Stroudley D1 class 0–4–2 tank no.2247 brings the Seaford 'motor' into Newhaven Harbour station in 1933, shortly before the branch was electrified. This station adjoined the railway's London & Paris Hotel – a fact that the nameboard acknowledges – and most local passengers for the cross-channel steamers used it to get to the marine platforms a little further on. On the right is the accumulator tower which once powered hydraulic equipment of all kinds throughout the port.
(Newhaven Local & Maritime Museum)

35. A rare picture of the original Bishop-stone station built to serve the Tide Mills village. The sparse shelters and gravel platforms were in keeping with the modest traffic it brought to the motor train on its way to Seaford behind a D1 tank. It closed for ever in 1942.
(Newhaven Local & Maritime Museum)

34. A pre-war boat train standing at the marine platforms after arriving from Victoria. To be exact the date is 11th October 1933 and the engine which was to become one of Newhaven's stalwarts is H1 class Atlantic no.2038 *Portland Bill*. This name was bestowed by the SR and celebrates, not a notorious convict but a headland on the coast served by the company. The engine's cab and boiler mountings can be compared with the cut down version used after 1935, seen in picture 11. Notice also the large bullseye headlamps of the old 'Brighton' pattern.
(Newhaven Local & Maritime Museum)

36. Standing at Seaford's single platform is a small Stroudley tank engine, ready to depart on a local service to Lewes. A Billinton van and three coaches will be quite enough for the traffic offering and there may be some significance in the fact that the goods shed on the right looks rather bigger than the station building, fronting the main road. But what is that putative greenhouse tacked onto the end of the station, behind the hedge? (Lens of Sutton)

Seaford Station.

38. The B4 class 4–4–0s succeeded the B2s and were considerable performers in their day though by 1930 they were mainly on secondary services like this Brighton - Hastings local, heading east out of Berwick. The engine is no.B54, and we can see some of the results of the 1923 grouping in the shape of the two leading carriages which are of LSWR origin. (Brighton Library)

37. We might think that Glynde's principal traffic was milk, by the number of churns on the platform and the cart from the Glynde Creameries just visible behind the name-board. In fact the station also served Firle and Beddingham as well as several nearby chalk pits. Only local trains called there and the one headed by a B2 class 4–4–0 on the up line is obviously a fast, disdaining Glynde. The platform seat is of the other common LBSCR pattern: compare with the one in picture 20. (Brighton Library)

London Brighton and South Coast Railway

Rudgwick to

Hassock's G.

39. The up loop at Polegate was a temporary resting place for the Hailsham train as it waited to make connections with up and down electrics on the East Coast line in June 1959. Such a powerful engine as a K mogul was not necessary, but merely filling in time between its goods duties. In the background is Polegate East signal box, while the original route of the Eastbourne branch is to the right of the camera.

40. The 1935 electrification brought many more trains to places like Hampden Park and the Southern Railway provided one of its standard concrete footbridges in place of the wicket gates beside the level crossing. It was a lot safer, if less convenient. In 1950 no.31891 was on a common weekend duty for a Maunsell mogul: a through train from the Western Region. (S.C. Nash)

←————

41. Eastbourne's second (1911) locomotive shed at the end of the 1940s was a Mecca for the knowing because it housed a collection of old LBSCR engines, a few at work and many in store but really waiting for the scrapyard. Some of them were optimistically steamed for the Christmas parcels workings and then retired to rust, while at least one was still in the pre-war green livery with gold numbers. I1X class 4–4–2 tank no.32005 had been active enough since 1947 to acquire the name of its new owners, unlike no.2054 behind it, which we last saw at Berwick, twenty years earlier in picture 38. (A.J.K. Wadmore)

42. Happier times for steam at Eastbourne with a B4 class (rebuilt to B4X) getting ready to leave for London about 1924, with an interesting selection of carriages. At the front is one of the brake vans from the 'Brighton' Royal train, followed by a Marsh high roofed bogie, an elderly Pullman, and what looks like a further pair of ex-Royals, with clerestories. This select gathering, the polish on the engine, and the man on the ladder doing some last minute cleaning seems to indicate the best train of the day, the 8.30am to London Bridge, which stopped only at Haywards Heath and slipped a portion for Victoria at East Croydon. Those were the days!

43. In Eastbourne, as in so many residential towns, the gasworks was the largest single user of coal and was connected to the main line railway system, straddling the line out to the ballast pit on the Crumbles, east of the town. The gasworks had its own engines and this one, *Mary*, was built by the Avonside Engine Co. of Bristol in 1909. (S.C. Nash)

UP.	Passngr.		Passngr.		Motor.		Passenger.		Passenger.		Motor.		Horse Boxes.		Passenger.				
	A.M.		A.M.		A.M.		A.M.		A.M.		A.M.				A.M.				
	arr.	dep.	arr.	dep.	arr.	dep.	arr.	dep.	arr.	dep.	arr.	dep.	arr.	dep.	arr.	dep.			
Hastings	...	...					...	8 15	...	...	...	...	...	...	...	...	...	...	...
St. Leon'ds, S.E.& C.R.	...	...					8 18	8 19	...	...	...	...			...	...	...	...	...
Bopeep Junction ...	...	...					...	8 21	...	...	...	...			...	...	...	...	...
St. Leonards *	...	...					8 22	8 23	...	...	...	...			...	...	...	...	...
Bexhill	...	...					8 29	8 30	...	...	...	...			...	...	...	...	...
Pevensey & Westham	...	...					...	...	...	...	...	...			...	...	...	...	...
Stonecross Junction	...	...	...	...			...	...	...	...	...	...			...	...	...	...	...
Hampden Park * ...	...	...	...	...			...	...	...	...	...	...			...	...	...	...	...
Eastbourne	...	...	...	8 30			...	...	...	...	...	...			...	...	...	...	...
Hampden Park *	...	...	...	8 34			...	...	...	...	...	...			...	...	...	...	...
Polegate	...	...	...	8 38			...	8 43	...	...	...	...			...	...	...	...	...
Berwick	...	...	...	...			...	...	...	...	...	...			...	...	...	...	...
Glynde	...	...	...	...			...	8 52	...	...	...	...			...	...	...	...	...
Southerham Junction	...	...	...	...			...	...	...	...	...	...			...	...	...	...	...
Lewes	...	...	K	8 51			8 58	9 2	...	...	...	9 9			...	...	...	...	...
Cooksbridge...........	...	...	...	...			...	...	...	...	9 15	9 16			...	...	...	...	...
Plumpton	...	...	...	...			...	...	...	...	9 22	9 23			...	...	...	...	...
Brighton	...	8 45	...	...			...	...	...	8 53	...	...			...	8 58	...	9 20	...
Preston Park	...	...	...	...			...	...	8 57	8 58	...	...			...	...	...	...	...
Hassocks............	...	...	...	...			...	...	9 9	9 10	...	...			9 14	9 20	...	...	...
Burgess Hill	...	...	...	...			...	...	9 15	9 17	...	...			9 30	9 38	...	...	...
Keymer Junction ...	...	9 0	...	9 4			...	9 16	...	9 18	...	9 30			...	9 40	...	9 35	...
Wivelsfield	...	...	...	...			...	...	9 19	9 20	...	...			...	...	...	...	...
Hayward's Heath ...	...	9 5	9 9	9 10			...	...	9 25	9 28	9 35	...			9 45	...	9 39	9 40	...
Balcombe............	...	...	...	...			9 25	9 26	9 35	9 36	...	...			...	...	...	...	...

Line from Balcombe Tnl. or Three Bridges ...	FAST		FAST		SLOW		FAST		SLOW				...		FAST				
Three Bridges.....		9 15		9 23	9 25	9 30	...	9 32	9 44	9 45	...	...			...	9 51	...	...	...
Gatwick		...		...	...	...	...	...	...	9 49	...	...			...	...	...	...	...
Horley		...		...	9 37	...	...	...	9 51	9 53	...	...			...	9 59	...	...	...
Earlswood		...		9 31	...	...	...	9 40	10 0	10 1	...	...			...	9 59	...	...	...
Thro' Line. {RedHill(Gds)		9 28		9 36	...	...	...	9 44	...	...	...	...			...	10 3	...	...	...
{Quarry																			
{Coulsdon *		9 33		9 40	...	...	...	9 49	...	...	...	...			...	10 8	...	...	...
Red Hill (Goods) ...		...		...	...	...	...	...	...	...	...	...			...	...	...	...	...
Red Hill Junction...		...		...	...	...	...	...	10 3	10 5	...	...			...	...	...	...	...
Coulsdon*		9 33		9 40	...	...	...	...	...	...	...	...			...	...	...	...	...
Purley		...		...	...	...	...	...	...	10 18	...	...			...	...	...	...	...
Local and Thro'. {Purley		...		...	...	...	...	9 51	...	...	...	...			...	10 10	...	...	...
{Purley Oaks		...		...	...	...	...	...	...	...	...	...			...	...	...	...	...
{S'th Croydon		...		...	...	...	...	...	...	...	...	...			...	...	...	...	...
{EastCroydon		...		...	...	...	...	9 56	...	...	...	...			...	10 15	...	...	...
South Croydon		...		...	...	...	...	...	...	...	...	...			...	...	...	...	...
East Croydon	P	9 39	P	9 46	...	...	...	...	10 22	10 24	...	...			...	...	...	...	...
Norwood Junction*...		9 41		9 48	...	...	...	9 59	...	...	...	...			...	10 18	...	...	...
Forest Hill	...	9 45	...	...	...	...	...	...	...	...	...	...			...	...	...	...	...
New Cross	...	...		9 55	...	...	...	...	...	...	...	...			...	10 25	...	...	...
Willow Walk	...	...	...	...	...	...	...	...	...	...	...	...			...	...	...	...	...
London Bridge	9 55	...	10 0	...	...	...	10 12	...	...	...	...	...			10 31	...	...	...	...
East Croydon		9 42		9 49	...	...	...	...	10 22	10 24	...	...			...	...	...	...	...

For Times at Intermediate Stations between East Croydon and Clapham Junction, see Local Pages.

| Clapham Junction ... | ... | 9 55 | 10 2 | 10 4 | ... | ... | ... | ... | 10 36 | 10 39 | ... | ... | | | ... | ... | ... | ... | ... |
| Victoria .... | 10 0 | ... | 10 10 | ... | ... | ... | ... | ... | 10 44 | | ... | ... | | | ... | ... | ... | ... | ... |

←

44. Pevensey & Westham station is actually in the latter place and has changed little since the 1950s when this train of seaborne coal from Newhaven to Galley Hill sidings at Bexhill rumbled through, behind one of Brighton's K class.

As well as showing two of the most important trains on the LBSCR, the 8.30am from Eastbourne and the 8.45am from Brighton to London Bridge (The City Limited) slipping their Victoria portions at East Croydon, this 1915 timetable also shows the 9.00am Motor from Horsham stopping at Gatwick to set down golfers. They would find it hard to get a game there today.

45. This unusual working is the weed-killing spray train being propelled towards Pevensey Bay Halt. It consists of 6 connected tank wagons, with a pair of vans in front doing the actual spraying and controlling affairs generally. The leading one carries the unusual combination of a headcode disc *and* a tail lamp. The South Downs beyond Polegate are visible above the train; Pevensey Castle just appears on the right; and the smokebox of yet another K class is about to eclipse our view of the whole scene.

46. One of the motor halts opened in 1905 was at Havensmouth Crossing, between Pevensey and Cooden, and was given the name Normans Bay Halt. The houses on the right are along the road at the back of the beach but the vicinity had not been developed as much as Pevensey Bay, so the Hastings to Brighton train approaching behind a B2X class 4–4–0 would not be stopping here. (Brighton Library)

Bexhill. L.B. and S.C.R. Station

47. This unlikely combination of an ex-LSWR class M7 tank and a train of GWR and BR carriages is working an equally unlikely duty: an excursion returning to Hailsham from Bexhill. Let us hope that the Hailsham residents benefited from the change of air. In the background is the one-time motor halt at Cooden, which was rebuilt as Cooden Beach in 1935. (J.J. Smith)

48. This old postcard view shows why good pictures of trains at Bexhill are rare: the site and the awnings make the station almost a tunnel. When these spacious facilities were provided early this century the residents were pleased, because the town's two previous stations had been unsatisfactory affairs, but now there was ample protection from the weather. (Brighton Library)

49. One of the 'Gladstone' class 0–4–2s is seen pulling away from Bexhill, with a train to Brighton in the 1920s. No.B619 began life in the striking Stroudley livery with the name *Cleveland* and as such appears in photo 25 of my *Steaming Through East Hants*, but by the time of this picture, it was nearing the end of its life. Note the addition of CENTRAL to the LBSCR nameboard by the Southern Railway. The new owners had two stations in Bexhill, and there must be no confusion. (A. Overbury collection)

50. Steam shed staffs were a versatile lot, and the gang at St. Leonards West Marina have borrowed the Brighton steam crane to lift the boiler out of B4 class no.58. The presence of a photographer may however suggest that it was not quite 'all in a day's work'. West Marina station is on the left with Bopeep Junction and the line from Tonbridge behind the camera.

51. Until 1931 Hastings only had one through platform (on the left) which was just adequate as most trains terminated there. The new station has four through platforms which allowed the electric services, which began in 1935, to run through to Ore where carriage sheds were built. This picture shows the old arrangement from the western end with the terminal platforms used by LBSCR trains on the right. From the carriages on the left, we can see why the SER had a consistently bad press. (Lens of Sutton)

52. This close-up shows 'Gladstone' no.B183 ready to leave the old Hastings station with a Brighton train in Southern Railway days. There is a train for London via Tonbridge on the left. Being an SER station the pattern of signals at Hastings was quite different from the LBSCR type with the flat cap finial. (Lens of Sutton)

3. The east end of the present Hastings
Station, taken through the lattice girders of
the footbridge in 1958. The new station is
partly on the site of the SER engine shed and
goods depot, the latter taking over part of the
site of the former terminal platforms. An
Ashford train is ready to leave behind an L
Class 4–4–0. (J. Powys/Hastings Library)

54. There is a considerable climb from Hastings up to Ore where the carriages of this excursion train will be cleaned and kept until it is time for the return home, so H class 0–4–4 tank no.31307 is assisting the 'Schools' which has brought them down from London. This practice ensured no delay, or worse – a train stalling and running back off the line at the catch points in the foreground. (J. Powys/Hastings Library)

55. In 1907 the SECR opened several halts
on the line from Hastings to Rye, just as the
LBSCR had done on the line to Eastbourne.
Steam railcars were used to reduce working
costs and the new service seems to have gen-
erated some extra business, as this 1909
picture of Three Oaks and Guestling Halt
shows. (Hastings Library)

56. A closer look at one of the SECR steam railcars, which has a large brass dome. In this scene at Snailham Halt, about 1910, we can see that an ordinary carriage has been added to the railcar. Is the young person on the footplate a boy who has just wheedled his way into such a coveted position? Snailham Halt closed in 1959. (Brighton Library)

57. When the railway first appeared at Rye in 1851 a swing bridge was provided over the river Rother, it being replaced by a fixed bridge in 1903. This picture shows the testing of the new bridge by running several engines coupled together over it. As usual such a rare happening has attracted a small army of workmen and officials. The nearest engine is a new D class 4–4–0, no.736, and the picture is by courtesy of Mr. Wickersham of Rye.

58. The SER liking for staggered platforms shows up well in this view of Rye taken in the 1950s. H class tanks with push and pull sets were the successors to the railcars. We can also see one of Mr. Tress' neo-classical station designs which, like the Hastings - Ashford line itself, has survived several closure attempts. (Lens of Sutton)

60. The fruits of the immediate success of the tramway are seen in this picture of a second engine – *Victoria*, another Bagnall – and next to it a second carriage built locally by the Rother Ironworks. With two engines and two carriages the Rye & Camber carried on until World War II. Alas it never reopened. These pictures were supplied by the late Miss B. Rhodes of Rye whose father is in both of them, driving the engine.

59. *Camber* at Camber Sands. This is the original loco of the Rye & Camber Tramway, built by Bagnalls of Stafford in 1895. The whole enterprise was so successful that its initial outfit of rolling stock had to be doubled within the first two years. Ten years later they even extended the line an extra half mile.

3. NORTH EAST SUSSEX: THREE BRIDGES TO HIGH ROCKS

This route across north Sussex has been pictured in *Branch Lines to East Grinstead* but all these views are different. East Grinstead has gone the full circle from branch terminus to bustling country junction to branch terminus again, but retains its rail link thanks to 'commuters', the American name for what traditional railwaymen called 'the business traffic'. More than that, hope is growing that the Bluebell Railway may push up from the south and give the town steam trains once more. But the east - west route is gone for ever and the latest news is that Ashurst Junction to Tunbridge Wells West has closed. Maybe that was inevitable once

the Brighton - Tonbridge link was broken, yet before 1914 Ashurst had no less than three slip coach services daily, Tunbridge Wells portions off London trains. Despite these historical marvels this north Sussex route was always one of the quietest LBSCR lines, though in fairness to the much maligned Southern Region, it was given its chance in the 1950s with an hourly service throughout the day. But it was places nearer London like Hurst Green, or on the electric services, like Hassocks, which grew. Maybe Hartfield and the rest are regretting their railway loss; maybe they are glad of their continuing quiet.

← ────────

61. Down the years the Three Bridges – East Grinstead service made do with engines and carriages which had seen better days, and the months before nationalisation were no exception. At that time the trains were usually of three coaches (two of which are under Three Bridges' over-all roof), but in later years a two coach push and pull set sufficed. The engine is E4 class 0–6–2 tank no.2520. (Brighton Library)

62. Rowfant station still stands among the woods of the Forest Ridge in north Sussex. It was built as the result of an agreement with a local landowner when the line was planned, there being no village nearby. The branch goods train had stopped there one summer's day in 1955 purely to pass a passenger train on the single line and not for traffic which, as the load of only four wagons shows, was very light. The engine amid the luxuriant vegetation was a 'Brighton' 0–6–0 of the C2X class, on its way home to Three Bridges.

63. Grange Road was the next station to Rowfant, and it too was struggling to keep nature at bay; indeed the tree in the background seems to have strayed from some tropical jungle. Although the station was named after a nearby mansion, a sprinkling of houses had appeared north of the line down the years, but despite the space between the track and the boundary fence, Grange Road never needed a passing loop or a second platform.

London Brighton and South Coast Railway.

Grange Road to

Balcombe.

64. A Three Bridges train leaving the High Level platforms at East Grinstead, with another C2X in charge of a 'Birdcage' or 'trio' set, rather than a rail motor. The Q class 0–6–0 at the other island platform is waiting to leave with the 1.05pm from Tunbridge Wells West to London Bridge via St. Margarets Junction and Oxted. Two varieties of SR signals are visible: lower quadrant on a concrete post is the early pattern, with the later upper quadrant type on the right. (S.C. Nash)

65. Before the BR Standard class 4 tanks arrived several of the LMS type of 2–6–4 tanks were used on the Oxted lines services, and here we see no.42066 arriving at Forest Row with a train from Victoria to Tunbridge Wells West. At one time this station was served by carriages slipped at Horley from the crack 5.05pm London Bridge to Eastbourne business train, but in 1955 those days were long gone.

66. Hartfield and Withyham must have been two of the quietest stations in East Sussex and pictures of steam trains at them are rare indeed, so this picture of Withyham's single platform must do for both. With so little for the staff to do, it was surprising that no effort was made to brighten the place up and qualify for an award in the Best Kept Stations competition. (H.C. Casserley)

←

67. Ashurst Junction signal box worked two junctions, one lying beyond it, where the lines from East Grinstead and Oxted via Edenbridge joined. The second junction, which we can see, died with the closure of the Groombridge and Tunbridge Wells line which this train from London is using, though the route on the left to Eridge via Birchden Junction remains open. The engine is U1 class no.31902; the signals apply to the East Grinstead (left) and Edenbridge lines. (J.H.W. Kent)

68. With so many services converging on Groombridge as the key to Tunbridge Wells, the route indicating discs carried by engines were vitally necessary. This one on the smokebox of a BR standard 2–6–4 tank means London - Tunbridge Wells via East Grinstead High Level, and the train is just passing Groombridge Junction signal box. The line to Birchden Junction and Eridge going off on the left completes the Ashurst - Groombridge - Eridge triangle. (J.H.W. Kent)

69. Because there was a lot of changing between trains at Groombridge the station was provided with an extra platform, on the right, where a connecting train could wait. Keen railwaymen added flowerbeds, common enough at country stations, and then surrounded them with a lawn, which was a great rarity. Beside these splendours, the 2–6–4 tank leaving for Eastbourne looks commonplace. (J.H.W. Kent)

6939 3rd - SINGLE . SINGLE - 3rd 6939
Uckfield to
Uckfield   Uckfield
Buxted   Buxted
BUXTED
(S) 6d H FARE 6d H (S)
For conditions see over For conditions see over

70. About 1958 the separate signal boxes at Groombridge station and Groombridge Junction were replaced by one modern box at the Tunbridge Wells end of the station. The block signalling instruments however remained the originals, seen in the upper right of this picture. They are Tyer's two position pattern, which required close attention for safe working, though things were made easier here by the use of track circuits showing on an illuminated diagram beside the signalman. (J.H.W. Kent)

71. Lonely High Rocks Halt between Groombridge and Tunbridge Wells saw few passengers and never had a frequent service of trains, for there was no village nearby. This is the platform for Tunbridge Wells, that for Groombridge being on the other side of the bridge from which this was taken. High Rocks was opened as one of the motor halts in 1907 and closed for ever in 1952. (Lens of Sutton)

4. EAST GRINSTEAD TO LEWES
The Sheffield Park line and the Plumpton line

My slender justification for lumping these two lines together is the one-time 8.07am from London Bridge. It's hard to believe, but this train – more of an expedition, given its slowness – ran through East Grinstead Low Level and Sheffield Park to Lewes, and then on via Plumpton and Haywards Heath back to Horsted Keynes. I think this was just the planners making use of the train once they had got it to Lewes, but what happened to it thereafter? They sent the poor thing back to Brighton via Haywards Heath again. Imagine falling asleep in that one at London Bridge after a night on the town!

The lines south of East Grinstead were of local inspiration, to improve communications with Brighton and Lewes, although in the end they were built and worked by the LBSCR. In no sense did they rival the main line, though until 1939 they were used in times of pressure as a relief route for slow steam excursions. They never were electrified, though it was promised at least twice. The nearest the third rail got was Haywards

72. This 1953 railtour, traversing several threatened branch lines, was one of the few passenger trains to use the single line connection from the Low Level to the High Level platforms at East Grinstead, referred to in *Branch Lines to East Grinstead* (Middleton Press). The line ran more or less parallel with the low level lines for much of its length. Notice the long brass grab handles at each door, a distinctive feature of LBSCR carriages.

Heath to Horsted Keynes, perhaps in the hope that the rest would follow piecemeal, or perhaps to give the Seaford - Haywards Heath trains somewhere quiet to reverse. Later came the troubled 1950s and all services were withdrawn from the steam lines. Copyhold Junction to Ardingly remains (to serve a roadstone depot), and so of course does Keymer Junction to Lewes, which originated to serve Newhaven and Hastings rather than Eastbourne or Lewes.

It was in the 1950s that the Brighton Evening Argus in a springtime feature article coined the term 'The Bluebell Line', which was adopted by those brave people who started and succeeded with Britain's first standard gauge preserved railway. Few of us gave much for their chances but they have flourished; let us wish them well in getting their line back to East Grinstead. But they'll never be able to run the old 8.07 from London Bridge.

73. Did the little 15 lever signal box at East Grinstead South date from the opening of the line in 1882, or had it previously seen service somewhere else in the changing pattern of East Grinstead layouts? The small windows above and weatherboarding below was certainly an early style and different from other boxes on the line. The early SR signal is of a type derived from LSWR practice. By the winter of 1957 the service to Lewes had shrunk to a tank engine and one coach, though the Three Bridges train at the High Level platform in the distance still has two coaches.

74. No.31823 was the first Maunsell mogul built by the SR and is seen leaving Kingscote with what looks like a Race Special from Brighton to Lingfield via East Grinstead. There is some useful timber traffic in the goods yard, but otherwise things at Kingscote are pretty quiet. It's washday in the station house.

75. Will West Hoathly station again resound to the magic of steam bursting out of the tunnel in the background and calling here on the way to East Grinstead? This train in April 1955 is the unlikely 3.28pm Haywards Heath to London Bridge, hauled by a K class 2–6–0 no.32344, but the signals give a false impression of traffic for the box was switched out with all the running signals left at clear. Beneath the one on the left is another which has a large letter S imposed upon it, with most of the green glass blanked off. When operated it allowed a down train to go forward a limited distance in order to get its tail into the goods yard at the other end of the station, the S indicating 'Shunt Ahead'.

76. Electric trains at Horsted Keynes used only the platform in the left foreground of this view of the north end of the layout. Steam trains using the Sheffield Park line called at the island platform which ended at the signal on the right, there being no direct connection to the electrified platform for them. Today these tracks go little further than we can see here, though if the Bluebell Railway succeeds in its efforts they will again go all the way to East Grinstead. The engine is an LMS type 2–6–4 tank no.42102, but the glorious signal is pure LBSCR.

77. After the second withdrawal of the East Grinstead - Lewes service in 1958 the line as far south as Horsted Keynes was still occasionally used for special traffic like this train headed by no.34068 *Kenley*, a Battle of Britain class light Pacific. It is just entering on the line to Ardingly and Haywards Heath which, though singled by 1959, was still used by the hourly trains to Seaford, which ran to and from a completely unsheltered platform behind this train. After several years the Bluebell Railway began to use the buildings and platforms we can see, for their service to Sheffield Park.

78. The branch goods pauses briefly at Ardingly to pick up folded wagon sheets lying on the platform beside the little signal box. The Stroudley tank engine has been caught by a Victorian photographer exactly between the ornate awning valances of this, one of the prettiest stations on the line. Behind the engine is an elaborate footbridge. (Brighton Library)

80. Pulling away from the main line at Keymer Junction, 'Schools' class no.30915 *Brighton* gets the 9.05am boat train from Victoria to Newhaven under way again after slowing almost to a stop for the severe check-railed curve. Enginemen and passengers are taking the air on a spring morning in 1954. The coaches are all SR except the leading one which is the last SECR Boat Train pattern.

79. In this view of a down Eastbourne express taken about 1930 we can see the double track from Horsted Keynes and Ardingly climbing up from the right to run beside the main line. The signal box is Copyhold Junction, opened in 1912 and closed on electrification in 1932. The train is headed by Eastbourne's U class no.A794, rebuilt by the SR from a 'River' class 2–6–4 tank, while the two leading coaches are D.E. Marsh's 'Balloon' or high roof type for the LBSCR, followed by a pair of Pullmans and some more 'Balloons'. The impressive run of point rodding in the foreground is to work the junction between the main line and the branch, out of sight to the right. (Lens of Sutton)

81. The last and most famous of the LBSCR Baltic tanks became the Company's War Memorial to its staff who fell in the first World War and was named *Remembrance*. Here, it is running into Plumpton with an up train from Eastbourne in 1934. The building behind the engine could date from the opening of the line in 1847, judging by the style of the Tudor hood moulds over the windows. (H.C. Casserley)

82. Cooksbridge as seen from the cab of a B4X class 4–4–0 working an up Newhaven boat train in 1937. Although there had been live rails here for electric trains since 1935, boat trains continued to be steam hauled into the 1950s. (H.C. Casserley)

83. After the present Lewes station was built, the former lines from the Plumpton direction were retained for goods trains avoiding the busy passenger station and giving direct access to Lewes Goods and East Yard. K class no.32347 is just entering these lines as it approaches from Haywards Heath. The direction of the rails indicates that the down island platform was built partly across the line of the earlier route.

84. During the pre-Bluebell era at Sheffield Park the 3.35pm Oxted to Brighton crossed the 4.03pm Lewes to Horsted Keynes. Both engines are taking water. The Southern Railway timetable of 1925 shows these same two trains running in the same timing and of course crossing here. In those days they would have been Stroudley D1 tanks with 'Brighton' bogies, but here we can see an LMS type 2–6–2 tank with SECR carriages, and a fine LBSCR signal.

85. Early Bluebell days at Sheffield Park with the LSWR 4–4–2 tank from Lyme Regis, the LNWR observation car from North Wales, and the 'Chesham' set from London. Also in the picture is an SECR high capacity third and the GWR 'Dukedog' no.9017. By 1963 when this view was taken, the Bluebell was well established, and in 1985 it celebrated its Jubilee of Steaming Through Sussex, making plans for a triumphal reopening north to East Grinstead in a few years time.

86. Newick & Chailey originally had an extensive layout with two platforms, a footbridge, goods yard and refreshment room, the last an attempt to make some money on an unremunerative line. A good view of these marvels when new is in picture 46 in *Branch Lines to East Grinstead*, but by June 1954 only the goods yard and the down platform got much regular use. In the local railway slang, this down train comprises a Teddy Bear pulling a Birdcage set.

88. The single line to Horsted Keynes and East Grinstead parted company with that to Eridge at Culver Junction, its rural ups and downs lying ahead of C2X class no.32434 as it accelerates away from us after picking up the train staff for the section. We can also see part of an LBSCR coach correctly carrying a side destination board reading EAST GRINSTEAD. Enginemen's protests at having to run tender first for 20 miles each trip eventually produced a tank engine which gave more shelter than a 'Vulcan' goods.

Barcombe Sussex.

87. When the passenger service on the Sheffield Park line was revived in the late 1950s it didn't call at Barcombe or Kingscote, but this old postcard recalls happier days with D3 class 0–4–4 tank no.373 at the platform with an up train. The station staff (and son) have turned out to be photographed beside the little signal box which, unusually, had its name high up under the eaves instead of at ganger's eye level. Compare this box with an older variety at East Grinstead South, picture 73. From its opening in 1882 until 1885, this station was called New Barcombe.

5. TWO ROUTES FROM ERIDGE
The Uckfield line and the Cuckoo line

The two lines going south from Eridge were very different. The Uckfield line was double track, pre-war it even had some semi-fast trains, and by the 1950s it was offering a regular interval service stopping at all stations but with many of the trains going through to Tonbridge to connect with South Eastern services. It started life as the Lewes & Uckfield Railway and grew an extension to Eridge and beyond under LBSCR ownership. Although several of the stations served only small villages there seemed to be useful traffic despite the parallel main road. The section between Eridge and Uckfield had to climb over the Forest Ridge, but the rest of the way to Lewes was level.

The Heathfield line was often called the Cuckoo line after the annual fair of that name at Heathfield. It was single track and had been opened in 1880 to keep the SER out of Eastbourne. Hailsham and Heathfield apart it served only villages, in a roundabout way with many steep gradients reflecting cheap construction through hilly country. Its sharp curves called forth a printed injunction in the LBSCR Working Timetable that 'Time must not be made up in running down inclines'. This was after a driver tried it once too often between Heathfield and Mayfield and was killed in the ensuing derailment. The line had two notable features in the natural gas plant at Heathfield (picture 100) and the electric tramway to the Asylum at Hellingly. These specialities, as well as some pretty scenery, contributed to an atmosphere of being more of a railway byway than the Uckfield line, which I hope these pictures capture. It was closed north of Hailsham in 1965, and completely in 1968, which was a sad loss for railway lovers.

89. Eridge was once quite a country junction, with four platforms arranged as two islands, where there were departures to Brighton, Eastbourne, Tunbridge Wells and London, but also periods of complete silence. This 1951 picture looking towards the up island shows a Brighton to Tunbridge Wells West train departing behind the first of the LBSCR 4–6–2 tanks, no.32325 formerly *Abergavenny*. The station buildings are on the bridge carrying the Uckfield - Tunbridge Wells road. The little wooden goods shed behind the engine didn't do much business. (S.C. Nash)

LONDON TO TUNBRIDGE WELLS, EAST GRINSTEAD, HORSTED KEYNES, HAYWARDS HEATH, LEWES AND BRIGHTON.—WEEK DAYS

Single Line between Culver Junc. and Horsted Keynes (Electric Train Staff). The Train Staff Stations are Culver Junc., Newick and Chailey, Sheffield Park and Horsted Keynes.

DOWN.	Passngr.		Passngr.		Passengr.		Passengr.		Passenger.		Passenger		Passngr.		Passenger	
					S O				**S O**							
	P.M		P.M.		P.M.		P.M.		P.M.		P.M.		P.M.		P.M.	
	arr.	dep.	arr	dep.	arr.	dep.	arr.	dep.	arr.	dep.	arr.	dep.	arr.	dep.	arr.	dep.
Victoria	...	...	...	2 25	...	2 35	...	...	...	...	...	3 45		Via Blue	...	...
Clapham Junction	...	...	2 31	2 33	...	2 41	...	...	...	...	...	3 51		Anchor.	...	...
	For Times at Intermediate Stations between Clapham Junction and East Croydon, see Local Pages.															
East Croydon	...	...	2 52	2 58	...	2 54						4 L 4	...	...	...	...
Willow Walk	...	...	...	...	...	...			...	2 57			...	...	...	4 10
London Bridge	...	...	...	...	...	...			...	3 0			...	...	...	...
South Bermondsey Junc.	...	...	...	...	...	...			...	3 4			...	...	...	...
New Cross	...	...	...	...	...	...			...	...			...	...	...	4 16
Forest Hill	...	...	...	...	...	...			...	...			...	...	...	4 25
Norwood Junction *	...	...	...	...	...	...			3 12	3 13			...	...	...	...
East Croydon	...	...	2 52	2 58	...	2 54			3 18	3 19		4 L 4	...	...	4 28	4 31
South Croydon	...	...	3 1	3 2	2 55	2 56			3 21	3 22		4 5	...	...	4 33	4 34
Selsdon Road Junction	...	...	3 3	3 4	...	...			3 24	3 25			...	...	4 36	4 37
Sanderstead	...	...	3 6	3 7	2 59	3 0			3 27	3 28			...	...	4 39	4 40
Upper Warlingham	...	...	3 14	3 15	3 6	3 7			3 35	3 36		4 12	...	...	4 47	4 48
Woldingham	...	...	3 19	3 20	...	...			3 40	3 41			...	...	4 52	4 53
Oxted	...	...	3 26	3 28	3 16	3 17		3 36	3 47	...	...	4 21	...	...	4 59	5 0
Hurst Green Junction Halt	...	...	...	3 30	...	3 19		3 38	...	...			...	...	...	5 2
Monks Lane Halt	...	...	...	...	...	...		...	...	...			...	...	...	...
Edenbridge Town	...	...	3 37	3 38	3 26	3 27		...	...	...			...	...	...	...
Hever	...	...	3 41	3 42	...	...		...	...	...			...	...	...	...
Cowden	...	...	3 46	3 47	3 34	3 35		...	...	...		P	...	...	...	...
Ashurst	...	...	3 52	3 53	...	3 39		...	...	...		4 33	4 34	4 37	...	...
Ashurst Junction	...	...	...	3 56	...	3 41		...	...	...		4 35	...	4 39	...	...
Groombridge	...	...	3 58	4 0	...	...		...	...	...			4 41	4 42	...	...
High Rocks Halt	...	...	...	...	...	...		...	...	...			...	...	...	...
Tunbridge Wells	...	...	4 6	...	...	...		...	...	...			4 48	...	...	...
Crowhurst Junction	...	...	...	...	...	...		3 41	...	...			...	...	...	5 5
Lingfield	...	...	...	...	...	...	3 46	3 47	...	...			...	...	5 9	5 10
Dormans	...	...	...	...	...	...	3 51	3 52	...	...			...	...	5 14	5 15
St. Margaret's Junction	...	...	...	...	...	...	...	3 56	...	...			...	...	...	5 19
East Grinstead (High Level)	...	...	...	...	...	...		...	...	...			...	...	...	...
East Grinstead (Low Level)	...	...	...	...	...	...	3 58		...	...			...	...	...	5 21
East Grinstead (Low Level)	...	3 0	*Passngr.*		...	...		Motor.					...	...	...	5 32
Kingscote	3 5	3 6			...	...							...	...	5 37	5 38
West Hoathly	3 10	3 11	P.M.		...	...		P.M.					...	...	5 43	5 44
Horsted Keynes	3 16	...	arr. dep.		...	...		arr. dep.					...	...	5 49	5 50
Horsted Keynes	...	3 17	...	4 0	...	...		...	...				...	...	...	...
Ardingly	3 22	3 23	4 5	4 6	...	...		...	...				...	...	...	...
Haywards Heath	3 28	...	4 12	...	...	...		...	...				...	...	...	...
Sheffield Park	...	...	...	...	...	...		...	...	4 35			...	...	5 59	6 3
Newick and Chailey	...	...	...	...	...	...		4 40	4 41				...	...	6 8	6 11
Barcombe	...	...	...	...	...	...		4 48	4 49				...	...	6 18	6 19
Culver Junction	...	...	...	...	...	...		4 52	4 53				...	...	6 22	6 23
Lewes	...	...	...	...	...	...		5 0	5 4				...	...	6 30	6 33
Falmer	...	...	...	...	...	...		5 13	5 14				...	...	...	...
London Road	...	...	...	...	...	...		5 19	5 20				...	...	6 47	6 48
Brighton	...	...	...	...	...	...		5 23	...				...	...	6 51	...

Column notes (printed vertically within the table):
- Calls Streatham Common and Thornton Heath.
- When this Train is running more than four minutes late, Oxted, Lingfield and Dormans must telegraph East Grinstead (Low Level) to say whether there are Passengers by it or not for the Three Bridges Train.
- Relief Line Norwood Junction North to South Croydon.
- Local Line Windmill Bridge Jc to South Croydon.
- Slip portion of 3.46 pm. Victoria.
- To Uckfield via Ashurst Spur. Through Carriages to Heathfield.
- To Brighton via Ashurst Spur. Through Carriages to Eastbourne. P Slips Tunbridge Wells Carriages at Ashurst.

In 1915 the premier 3.45pm from Victoria, disdaining East Croydon and Oxted, served Tunbridge Wells by slip coach at Ashurst.

LONDON TO TUNBRIDGE WELLS WEST, EAST GRINSTEAD, SHEFFIELD PARK, HEATHFIELD & UCKFIELD LINES.

DOWN. WEEK-DAYS.	Pass. p.m. arr.	dep.	Pass. p.m. arr.	dep.	Pass. p.m. arr.	dep.	Pass. p.m. arr.	dep.	N.S. Pass. p.m. arr.	dep.	Motor. p.m. arr.	dep.	N.S. Pass. p.m. arr.	dep.	Pass. p.m. arr.	dep.	Pass p.m. arr.	dep.	Pass. p.m. arr.	dep.	Mtr. p.m. dep.
VICTORIA	...		...	3 45	...	...			...	...		...			...	...		4 50			
Clapham Junc.																					
CHARING CROSS					...	...													...		
Waterloo Junction	...																				
CANNON STREET						4 10	4 19	4 20						4 37							
LONDON BRIDGE	...	...	...	...			4 16								...						
South Bermondsey Jct.							4 14														
Bricklayer's Arms Jct.	...	...					4 16	4 25					4 42								
New Cross Gate	...							4 31													
Forest Hill	...												4 54	4 56							
Norwood Junc.																					
Windmill Bridge Jct.	...		4	3				4 27	4 28	4 31	4 38	4 40	4 37		4 59				5 7		
East Croydon			4	4			4 33	4 34	4 42	4 43			5 0	5 2		5 8	5 10				
South Croydon	...								4 45	4 46											
Selsdon Road Junc.							4 37	4 38	4 48	4 49						5 15	5 16				
Sanderstead							4 45	4 46	4 55	4 56						5 22	5 23				
Upper Warlingham			4 12				4 50	4 51	5 0	5 1						5 27					5 40
Woldingham	...						4 57	4 58	5 7	5 9			5 19	5 21		5 34	5 36				5 43
Oxted									5 0							5 38					
Hurst Green Halt	...		4 22					5 0	5 11				5 23								
Hurst Green Junc.																					
Monks Lane Halt							5 18	5 19					5 30	5 31		5 45	5 46				
Edenbridge Town							5 22	5 23								5 49	5 50				
Hever							5 27	5 28								5 54	5 55				
Cowden							5 33	5 34					5 43			6 0	6 1		6 5		
Ashurst			P 4 37	P	4 38	4 41		5 37								6 4			6 8		
Ashurst Junc.			4 39		4 43													6 10	6 11		
Groombridge	...		...		4 45	4 46	5 39	5 40													
High Rocks Halt																	6 17				
T'B'DGE WELLS WEST					4 52		5 46														
Crowhurst Junc.								5 3										Pass. p.m. arr. dep.	5 52		
Lingfield							5 7	5 10											5 57		
Dormans							5 14	5 15													
St. Margarets Junc.																					
E. GRINSTEAD (H.L.)																			6 4		
E. GRINSTEAD (L.L.)	...		...				5 21	5 35													
Kingscote							5 40	5 41													
West Hoathly							5 46	5 47									6 28				
Horsted Keynes							5 51	5 53													
Ardingly																6 33	6 34				
Copyhold Junc.																6 37					
Haywards Heath					Pass. p.m. arr. dep.											6 40					
Sheffield Park }S	...		...		6 2	6 10															
Newick & Chailey }	...		...		6 15	6 20															
Barcombe }					6 27	6 28															
T'B'DGE WELLS WEST			...		4 25						5 8	5 9				5 50					
High Rocks Halt					4 31	4 33					5 12	5 13									
Groombridge					4 36						5 15		5 44		5 56	5 57					
Birchden Junc.			4 40		4 38	4 49									6 0		6 5				
Eridge			4 42	4 45	4 51	4 52					5 17	5 18	5 46	5 48	6 2	6 10	6 7	6 14			
Redgate Mill Junc.			4 48										5 50		6 12	6 13	6 12				
Rotherfield					4 56	4 57									6 17	6 18					
Mayfield					5 5	5 7									6 26	6 27					
Heathfield }					5 19	5 27									6 38	6 39					
Waldron }S					5 35	5 36									6 47	6 48					
Hellingly }					5 44	5 45									6 56	6 57					
Hailsham }		5 24			5 49	5 51									7 1	7 2					
Polegate	5 31	5 33			5 58	6 1									7 9	7 15					
Hampden Park	5 37	5 38			6 5	6 6									7 20	7 21					
EASTBOURNE	5 42				6 10										7 25						
Crowborough			4 52	4 54							5 25	5 26	5 55	5 56			6 21	6 22			
Buxted			5 3	5 4							5 35	5 36	6 5	6 6			6 31	6 32			
Uckfield			5 8	5 10							5 40		6 10				6 36	6 38			
Isfield			5 15	5 15													6 43	6 44			
Barcombe Mills			5 21	5 22													6 49	6 50			
Culver Junc.			5 24				6 31	6 32									6 52				
Lewes	...		5 30	5 32			6 39	6 46									6 58	7 0			
Falmer			5 45	5 46			7 0	7 1									7 9	7 17			
London Road, Brighton	...						7 4										7 15	7 16			
BRIGHTON	...		5 49														7 19				

Down — **Week Days**—*continued*

Station							p.m		p.m	p.m	p.m		p.m		p.m					p.m
Victoria ... dep							2 48		3 48	3 52	3 52		4*16		4 25					4*16
Clapham Junction "							2U53		3 53				4U*22							4U*22
London Bridge "						2SX31			3931	3851	3851	4 18	4 20		4*20					4 20
New Cross Gate "																				
East Croydon dep							3 5		4 5	4U9	4U9	4 35	4 39		4 40					4 42
South Croydon												4 38								4 46
Selsdon																				
Sanderstead												4 42								4 50
Riddlesdown												4 46								4 54
Upper Warlingham												4 52								5 0
Woldingham												4 57								5 5
Oxted arr										4 25	4 25	5 4	4 56							5 12
Oxted dep										4 25	4 25									5 13
Hurst Green Halt																				5 16
Monks Lane Halt																				
Edenbridge Town										4 35	4 35									5 25
Hever																				5 28
Cowden																				5 33
Ashurst										5 4	5 4									5 38
Groombridge 239 & below																				5 45
High Rocks Halt																				
Tunbridge Wells West arr										5U11	5U11									5 52
Ashurst dep																				
Eridge (below) arr										4 50	4 50									
Oxted dep	3 35							4 10				5 4	4 56							
Hurst Green Halt	3 37							4 12				5 8	4 59							
Lingfield	3 46							4 21				5 17	5 8							
Dormans	3 51							4 26				5 21	5 13							
East Grinstead 239 arr	3 58							4 33				5 28	5 20							
Three Bridges dep							3 48		5 9						5 9					
Rowfant							3 54		5 15						5 15					
Grange Road							3 58		5 19						5 19					
East Grinstead 239 arr							4 4		5 26						5 26					
East Grinstead dep							Stop	4 33	5 32						5 32					
Forest Row								4h46	5 39						5 39					
Hartfield								4 54	5 47						5 47					
Withyham								4 58	5 50						5 50					
Groombridge 239 & below								5 7	5 58						5 58					
High Rocks Halt								5 14												
Tunbridge Wells West arr								5 18	6 6						3 6					
East Grinstead dep	3 59											5 30	5 30		Stop					
Kingscote	4 5											5 37	5 37							
West Hoathly	4 10											5 43	5 43							
Horsted Keynes	4 16											5 49	5 49							p.m
Horsted Keynes dep		4 17	4 23		4 45	4 45								6 0		6 0	6 16	6 16		6 40
Ardingly		4 21	4 27		4 50	4 50								6 4		6 4	6 20	6 20		6 44
Haywards Heath 197 { arr		4 25	4 31		4 56	4 56	p.m							6 8		6 8	6 24	6 24		6 49
{ dep		4 28		4 33	4 59	5 15	5 5							6 13		6 17	6 23	6 28	6 33	6 35	6 56
Wivelsfield		4 32			5 5	5 9											6 32	6 38			7 2
Burgess Hill		4 35			5 8	5 12									6 23		6 35	6 40			7 6
Hassocks		4 39			5 12	5 16									6 27		6 39	6 44			7 10
Preston Park		4 47			5 20	5 24									6 35		6 37	6 47			7 14
Brighton 159 arr		4 50			5 23	5 27								6 29	6 39		6 41	6 50	6 55		7 17
Sheffield Park	4 29				Stop	Stop						6 4	6 4							
Newick and Chailey	4 34						p.m					6 12	6 12							
Barcombe	4 42											6 21	6 21							
Tunbridge Wells West dep							4 35													
High Rocks Halt																				
Groombridge (above)							4 42													
Eridge (above)							4 47		4 52	4 59										
Crowboro' & Jarvis Brook									4 59											
Buxted									5 9											
Uckfield									5 14											
Isfield									5 20											
Barcombe Mills									5 26											
Lewes 158, 197	4 53				4 50	5 16			5 34			6 37	6 37						6 51	7 1	
Falmer	5 9								5 50			6 52	6 52							
London Road (Brighton)	5 13								5 54			6 56	6 56							
Brighton 159 arr																				
Rotherfield and Mark Cross	Stop								Stop	5 7	Stop									
Mayfield										5 17										
Heathfield										5 30										
Waldron and Horam	p.m									5 38										
Hellingly	4 31					p.m			p.m	5 46	p.m									
Hailsham	4 36				5 21	p.m			5 44	5 52	6 50									
Polegate 158, 197	4 46				5 28	5 33			5 51	6 5	6 57									
Hampden Park	4 50					5 37			5 56	6 11	7 2								7 14	7 27	
Eastbourne arr	4 54			5 11	5 41	5 41			6 1	6 16	7 7								7 14	7 27	

In 1925 the same train was non-stop to Eridge, and still slipping a portion at Ashurst. By 1948 all slip coach services had disappeared, the departure time from Victoria had gone back 10 mins., and passengers for Tunbridge Wells had to change at Eridge.

90. From 1868 to 1880 this station was called Rotherfield but then lost its name to the new one on the Heathfield line, being renamed Crowborough. Jarvis Brook was added in 1897 when the Eridge to Uckfield line was doubled, the present station being built a few years later. This picture dates from just before the rebuilding and shows a train bound for Lewes arriving behind a Stroudley 2–2–2. (Lens of Sutton)

91. The line from Lewes to Uckfield was opened in 1858 by the Lewes & Uckfield Railway but its extension through Buxted to Eridge and Tunbridge Wells was not completed by the LBSCR for another ten years. Unlike the Lewes - Uckfield section it still has trains. The engine in this Edwardian postcard is rather a rarity: no.466, one of only four members of the ubiquitous E4 class 0–6–2 tank to be rebuilt with a large boiler, making class E4X. (Lens of Sutton)

92. Spring is in the air at Uckfield as the N class mogul runs in from Eridge; the trees are still bare but the door and window of the signal box are wide open to the sunshine. It has a gate wheel for the busy level crossing at the foot of the High Street. No question of working these gates by hand, as at Barcombe Mills, even though the train service was much the same there.

93. Besides the train from Tonbridge this picture shows the staple of many a country goods yard, the truckload of coal for local fireplaces. The engine is one of the SECR class L, built by Beyer Peacock of Manchester in 1914, just in time for the troop trains to France, and is seen here north of Isfield station, 40 years later. Today steam still runs over these rails for they are part of the Lavender Line, Isfield's own preserved railway.

94. Barcombe Mills station took its name in 1885 from the nearby watermills on the river Ouse, after the other station about a mile away on the Sheffield Park line lost its prefix 'New' (photo 87). The signal box beside the level crossing was erected in 1878 and at one time controlled access to a siding that branched off behind the train to serve the corn mill. Unlike those across busier roads, these gates were hand worked by the signalman who had to come out of his box twice for every train.

95. Culver Junction signal box was provided when the Sheffield Park line was opened in 1882 and changed little down the years until it was finally closed in 1958. The Tonbridge to Brighton train headed by D1 class no.31470 is accelerating briskly from Barcombe Mills station in the background, its last stop before Lewes. In the foreground between the rails we can see the plunger of the facing point lock which proved the points were properly set one way or the other, while to the left of the track is another piece of equipment which made sure that only the signal corresponding to the lie of the points could be cleared.

96. A close look at picture 52 in *South Coast Railways – Brighton to Eastbourne* will detect the line to Uckfield rising steeply to cross Lewes High Street. When the present station was built this line was given a new and more curved alignment going off to the right in this picture. It was taken from the chopped-off bridge abutment to which the previous line once climbed, coming in on the left as indicated by the curving brick wall. The buildings are on the far side of Lewes High Street and the train, like so many 1950s Tonbridge - Brighton services, is completely former SECR stock.

97. A vintage 1950 scene at Redgate Mill Junction signal box, the Heathfield line going off on the right, whither this train is bound. The engine is one of the E5 class 0–6–2 tanks, the passenger version of E4, and this is no.32404, visually little altered since building in 1904. The weatherboarded signal box is not thought to be one of the 'stilts' variety, but built in timber on the edge of an embankment where a brick structure might have had problems. The signalman is out by the steps, holding aloft the single line train staff, and behind him are the fire buckets going up the steps like 'pretty maids all in a row'.
(S.C. Nash)

98. Rotherfield & Mark Cross was the first station down the line, with a signal box more typical of the branch. On 25th October 1950 the 10.42am from Tunbridge Wells West was powered by one of the LMS type 2–6–4 tanks which had recently arrived on the scene. The station was of the pattern virtually standard for the branch: main buildings on the 'road' side and a matching shelter on the opposite platform. (S.C. Nash)

99. The 1.45pm from Eastbourne to Sevenoaks was timetabled to cross a train from Tunbridge Wells at Mayfield but for safe working on the single line no.80147 had to stop at the home signal in the background until the late running down train had come to rest in the platform loop line. Then it was allowed into the up platform loop and here we see it making a noisy and impatient entrance. By 1957 Mayfield station's original oil lamp standards were enjoying the benefits of Sugg's swan-neck conversion to gas.

100. Mayfield station was lit by coal gas, but Heathfield's supply was once more exotic. Natural gas was discovered when the railway was drilling for water in 1896 and after some hesitation was used to light the station and a few street lamps. The gas was also bottled for sale and this 1957 picture shows the site of the find, with the tiny gas holder. There is also an elevated water tank to supply the platform water cranes with the gas bottling establishment in the brick structure beneath. The whole matter enjoyed some local fame for many years. Beyond is Heathfield tunnel which had but a single running line in it, the left hand track leading only to a sand drag by 1957, though formerly it went right through the tunnel and out the other end to buffer stops.

102. Hellingly was the only station on the Heathfield line without a loop where trains could pass each other. The tracks behind 2-6-4 tank no.42103 were for the traffic of the electric tramway to the Mental Asylum, which ran behind the fence in the background. At one time there was a platform for passengers alongside the main running line but that service ceased in 1931. A picture of the antique electric locomotive appears in *Industrial Railways of the South East* (Middleton Press), photo 59. Note the typical Myres awning supports in carved timber.

←————————

101. The name of T.H. Myres is now associated with the architecture of the stations built on the Heathfield and Sheffield Park lines in the early 1880s, and Horam is typical of them. It is in the cottage style with red brick and tiles, a charming 'little brother' matching the main building. An up train from Eastbourne is crossing the down goods which is waiting to get to the goods yard in the distance. The guard's van is painted grey to show that it has no continuous brake, but at least it is properly displaying side lamps as well as a tail lamp. At night the driver could look back for their assurance that none of his train had broken away and been left behind.

2nd · SINGLE   SINGLE · 2nd

1699

Heathfield to

Heathfield   Heathfield
Rotherfield & M.C.   Rotherfield & M.C.

ROTHERFIELD & MARK CROSS

(S)   1/2 FARE   1 2 0   (S)

For conditions see over   For conditions see over

1699

103. In early Victorian times Hailsham was at least as important as Eastbourne and got its branch from Polegate at the same time, in 1849. For 31 years it remained a terminus and eventually between 1965 and 1968 reverted to that status. But from 1880 to 1965 it was a through station, though many of its trains were only 'shorts' from Eastbourne, as is this one. We are at the north end of the station with the little North signal box down below, the single line to Hellingly commencing a few yards behind us. The original Tudor style buildings are above the engine, the awning and this platform being a later addition. E4 class no.32475 has not come 22½ miles, because the mile post reads from Brighton via Lewes, the original route to Hailsham.

104. A last look at the Cuckoo line in 1959, as a K class pulls away from the 1881 station at Polegate with a Hailsham train. The original line to Hailsham crossed this line at right angles from right to left by the distant water tank, as it swung round to the north to join the later route about ¼ mile further north. The signal box in the distance is Polegate West.

London Brighton & South Coast Railway,

District Superintendent's Office.

Brighton May 23rd 1896

Mr F Blew
Copthorne
Near Crawley

Sir/.

Please go to Hailsham
first train on Saturday
next 23rd Instant as
Porter 14/5 per week,
reporting yourself to
Mr Read Stn Master
on arrival.
        I enclose pass
from Grange Road Stn
        Yours truly
            F Buckskin.

6. THE HASTINGS LINE

For those who remember the last generation of steam, the Hastings line will always be associated with the 'Schools' class. These powerful and competent 4–4–0s were not designed specially for the line but proved to be ideal engines to cope with the gradients encountered in crossing the Weald of Sussex. The difficulties of operating the Hastings line were aggravated by clearance problems in the tunnels, shoddy work by the original contractors being the cause. When their shortcomings were discovered it was found that not only was the brick lining of some of the tunnels inadequate, but also that it was possible to crawl the whole length of the tunnel in a void between the brickwork and the ground through which the structure was bored. They were strengthened by adding rings of brickwork to the linings, so reducing the space for trains. This didn't matter much in the days of small engines and rolling stock, but when the SR wanted to use carriages of modern dimensions, they wouldn't fit, and specially narrow vehicles had to be designed. They first ran in 1929, lasting to the end of steam, and as the 'Schools' class engines with round-topped fireboxes also cleared the Hastings line structure gauge, a new standard formation was created for the route.

By comparing these pictures with the rest

we can discern some characteristic differences between the SER and the LBSCR. For one thing the former was very keen on stations with staggered platforms, and there were other detailed differences like the shape of an awning valance, a signal post finial, or the base of a platform seat. In one respect the stations in this chapter are not typical of the SER: they forsake the weatherboard style it loved. That is because they were mostly designed by one man, William Tress, and have an Italian/classical style, with round-headed windows, deep eaves, and gently pitched roofs. The notable exceptions are Mountfield Halt, in the best 'old sleeper' style, and Bexhill West which was built half a century after the others, in Edwardian Baroque style. This was as typical of the SECR way of doing things – with a splash – as penny-pinching weatherboarding was of the old SER.

This chapter also includes some pictures of that Sussex outpost of the empire of Col. Holman F. Stephens, the Rother Valley section of his Kent & East Sussex Railway, which had a style of its own, and not only as regards buildings. Its trains and its operating methods were quite different from anything else in this book as I hope you can see from the pictures. At present the reborn KESR doesn't run regularly into Sussex, but I'm sure they will before long and we will all be able to experience steaming through the Rother Valley at first hand. Not so on the Hastings line which has had its distinctive brand of diesels (those tunnels again) for over 20 years, but now they too are on their way out, for the all-conquering Southern Electric is coming.

105. The little signal box at Frant, squashed into a narrow space at the north end of the down platform, has a fair portion cantilevered out over emptiness. Also presented for our inspection are some choice platform lamps and the 12.16pm Victoria to Hastings storming through behind no.30916 *Whitgift*. The corrugated erection beyond the signal box stored oil for the station and signal lamps.

106. The Hastings line never had a lot of goods traffic which was probably just as well, given its gradients. But in the Q1 class 0–6–0 the Southern had engines totally masters of the job as no.33031 demonstrates, pounding up the gradient into Wadhurst with a train that stretches down the bank and round the corner out of sight. This class was associated with the line from 1948 until the diesels came in 1962. The signal in this 1957 view is Wadhurst's up home, on a typical Southern Railway gantry made of old rails.

107. Stonegate station was called Ticehurst Road until 1947 and is the work of William Tress in his Italianate neo-classical style. It is half way down the eight mile bank from Wadhurst to Etchingham with the result that despite some sharpish curves no.30924 *Haileybury* with Bulleid's large chimney was moving the 2.25pm Charing Cross to Hastings at high speed. The signal box, like Frant's, is placed at the conjunction of the staggered platforms. Leading the carriages is one of the last SECR corridor 'birdcage' brakes in red and cream, with some 1921 boat train stock following.

108. At the bottom of the bank from Wadhurst another 'Schools' no.30908 *Westminster* tears round the curve through Etchingham with the 10.25am Charing Cross to Hastings on 24th April 1957. The ride in the leading end of the 1921 SECR high capacity third class coach must have been distinctly lively. Non-corridor vehicles like this were pressed into service on summer Saturdays to augment popular trains, each one providing no less than 100 seats in 10 compartments.

109. This picture at Robertsbridge presents an interesting contrast with the view of Stonegate because although the design of the building is similar, Robertsbridge has had less attention paid to its architectural detail and looks quite ordinary. The rather slab-sided corridor coaches seen here were built for this line because of the clearance problem. In fact the 3.25pm from Charing Cross was as near as one could get to a standard formation for a Hastings fast train. By 1957 when this picture was taken there had been no connections to Tenterden for nearly four years and no 'Terrier' waiting in the bay behind this train.

110. Times past at Robertsbridge with the Kent & East Sussex branch train waiting in the bay for any traffic off the down 'stopper' which followed the fast from London. The Stroudley 'Terrier' has been fitted with a Drummond chimney and the brake composite behind is also of LSWR origin. When this picture was taken in the winter of 1953 the service to Tenterden was already doomed. Note the outsize platform nameboard on the right, advising passengers to change for the KESR line, and also the coupled chimney-stacks on Mr. Tress' station building. Was he a pupil of Sir William Tite who, as readers of *Steaming Through East Hants* will know, was partial to this feature?

111. 'Hope springs eternal . . .' Hawkhurst was at least four miles from Junction Road Halt which got its name from being at the level crossing over the 'junction' turnpike from Hastings to Hawkhurst. The platform seems to have been modernised but the sign is genuine KESR. The well coaled 'Terrier' is again no.32678, but I can hardly believe there was just no room on the footplate for the bucket, which therefore had to be hung on a lamp iron. A goods brake completes the train to Robertsbridge which will run 'mixed' on its return journey.

112. Confession time. Because there were so few trains on the KESR I had to ask the driver to linger over his call at Bodiam station to give me time to negotiate the cattle grid and get my picture of the departing train. Photography of branch line trains posed many problems but lack of co-operation by railway staff was not often one of them. At the more out of the way places, lonely railwaymen positively encouraged one to linger and chat.

113. The seeming bustle of activity at Northiam on 28th November 1953 was, alas, the prelude to the end of passenger trains a few weeks later. This train has a 'birdcage' brake carriage instead of the LSWR coach, but the station buildings in corrugated sheet could almost be described as 'Col. Stephens Standard'. Is it too much to hope that one day the efforts of Kent & East Sussex Railway enthusiasts will again bring passengers to its platform and even replace the long vanished one beyond the loop line?

114. Back on the main line we find Mountfield Halt which was in rather a quiet part of the Sussex Weald and looked antique, but was in fact a Southern Railway creation. Its sleeper platforms and oil lamps didn't prosper and BR closed it in 1969, though not before the last SECR class E 4–4–0 called with the 'stopper' from Tonbridge to Hastings. Engine no.31166 was built in 1907 but the carriages are Southern of 1934.

116. Crowhurst Park Siding grew into Crowhurst Junction at the turn of the century when the SECR opened the branch to Bexhill. The new station was of the SER pattern with through lines in the centre for fast trains and platform loops for those which did stop, like the 5.25pm Charing Cross to Hastings. The signals show there was provision for through running onto the branch, though locals to Bexhill had bay platforms of their own outside the main line ones. It was an elaborate layout which business probably never justified. The 'Schools' class, with its straight-sided carriages is no.30932 *Blundells*, known by its unique high-sided tender.

→

025

SOUTHERN RAILWAY.
Available for TWO
MONTHS.   (SEE BACK)

Charing Cross to

ROBERTSBRIDGE

(T) First Class 2 1/2

SOUTHERN RAILWAY.
Available DAY of Issue
ONLY.   (SEE BACK)

Robertsbridge to

CHARING CROSS

2 1/2 First Class (T)

025

115. As a change from the frequent 'Schools', let us admire the polish on an L1 class, no.31786, as it calls at Battle on a summer afternoon. We can also notice the distinctive awning valance which was an SER/SECR standard detail, and the letters SER in the base of the platform seat.

117. The new junction had a substantial signal box which is a check list of SER details: weatherboarded, hipped roof, sash windows, and a railed gallery for cleaning them. By 1957 branch services were usually provided by a pull-and-push set, here being propelled across the line to Hastings by H class 0–4–4 tank no.31162. Although it was late April, the English spring weather demanded steam heating for the train. Picture no.116 was taken from beside the spare branch coaches on the right.

118. Sidley was the only intermediate station on the branch and less than a mile from Bexhill itself which had grown out to take over the erstwhile village. The station there was in a cutting with the main buildings at street level, its platforms reached by a considerable footbridge. In this view a train from Crowhurst is slowing to a stop controlled by the driver in the leading end of a 1913 SECR coach, with the fireman alone on the footplate of the engine.

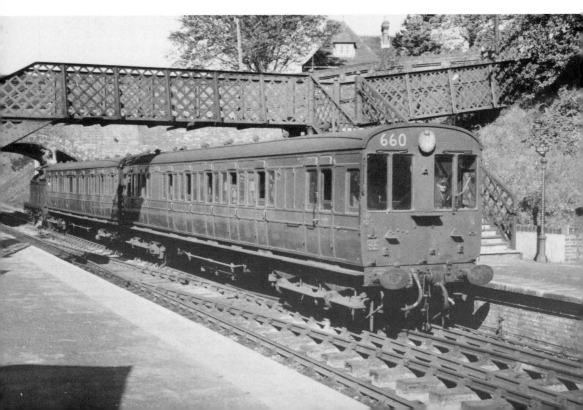

119. The Southern Railway renamed the branch terminus Bexhill West in 1923 to avoid confusion with the station on the East Coast line. It had two spacious covered island platforms with an engine release line between, controlled by a separate signal box at its head, beside the concourse. This was fronted by some lavish Edwardian Baroque buildings with which the SECR hoped to make its presence felt in Bexhill. What happened to those high hopes is summed up by the two coach motor train in this picture. At least two of the other platforms were stabling empty stock, the nearer one holding a new diesel train due into service in June 1957.

120. Steam workings off the Tonbridge line had to be fitted into the coastwise electric service at Bopeep Junction, St. Leonards, which is behind the camera, and this picture shows the 4.07pm all stations train from Sevenoaks waiting at the down platform of West St. Leonards for the slow electric (4.14pm from Brighton) to clear Warrior Square. It was taken just before the diesel trains started on the Hastings line, though it would appear from the concrete 'harps and slabs' by the engine that platform lengthening was still in progress. Time marches on and the platforms were rebuilt again in August 1985 in readiness for electrification.

MP Middleton Press

BRANCH LINES
Vic Mitchell and Keith Smith

BRANCH LINES TO MIDHURST	0 906520 01 0
BRANCH LINES TO HORSHAM	0 906520 02 9
BRANCH LINE TO SELSEY	0 906520 04 5
BRANCH LINES TO EAST GRINSTEAD	0 906520 07 X
BRANCH LINES TO ALTON	0 906520 11 8
BRANCH LINE TO HAYLING	0 906520 12 6
BRANCH LINE TO SOUTHWOLD	0 906520 15 0
BRANCH LINE TO TENTERDEN	0 906520 21 5
BRANCH LINES TO NEWPORT	0 906520 26 6

SOUTH COAST RAILWAYS
Vic Mitchell and Keith Smith

BRIGHTON TO WORTHING	0 906520 03 7
WORTHING TO CHICHESTER	0 906520 06 1
CHICHESTER TO PORTSMOUTH	0 906520 14 2
BRIGHTON TO EASTBOURNE	0 906520 16 9
RYDE TO VENTNOR	0 906520 19 3

SOUTHERN MAIN LINES
Vic Mitchell and Keith Smith

WOKING TO PORTSMOUTH	0 906520 25 8

STEAMING THROUGH
Peter Hay

STEAMING THROUGH KENT	0 906520 13 4
STEAMING THROUGH EAST HANTS	0 906520 18 5
STEAMING THROUGH EAST SUSSEX	0 906520 22 3

OTHER RAILWAY BOOKS

INDUSTRIAL RAILWAYS OF THE SOUTH-EAST	0 906520 09 6
WAR ON THE LINE The official history of the SR in World War II	0 906520 10 X
GARRAWAY FATHER AND SON The story of two unique railway careers.	0 906520 20 7

OTHER SUSSEX BOOKS

MIDHURST TOWN – THEN & NOW	0 906520 05 3
EAST GRINSTEAD – THEN & NOW	0 906520 17 7
THE GREEN ROOF OF SUSSEX A refreshing amble along the South Downs Way.	0 906520 08 8
THE MILITARY DEFENCE OF WEST SUSSEX	0 906520 23 1
WEST SUSSEX WATERWAYS	0 906520 24 X